This journal is for couples who want to work through
the interpersonal issues they are experiencing by being together.

Couple's Journey

For Couples Who Care

A Journal to Help Couples Grow In Love & Respect

Tony Cubito, M.A.
Cristi Cubito, M.A.

Blue Pearl Publishing Company

Table of Contents

Dedication

We would like to dedicate this journal to all the couples we have worked with from whom we have learned so much.

May all their hard work, which has helped so greatly in this body of work, be of service to other couples who are struggling to understand their own relationships.

Couples Journey
For Couples Who Care
A Journal to help couples grow in love and respect
Tony Cubito, M.A. and Cristi Cubito, M.A.

Published by:
Blue Pearl Publishing Company
P.O. Box 50248
Eugene, OR 97405
United States
www.couplesjourney.com

Library of Congress Cataloging-in-Publication
Cubito, Tony and Cristi
Couples Journey: For Couples Who Care/A Journal to help
couples grow in love and respect
Paperback ISBN no. 0-9715585-0-7
Library of Congress Catalog no. 2001119549

Printed in the United States of America

Cover artwork:
The Flower Speaks cards created by:
Marlene Rudginsky

Cover and text design by:
Marilyn Ditto

ACKNOWLEDGEMENTS

We have received so much help and encouragement from so many people. Marlene Rudginsky, who so artfully created the picture of the swans on the cover, has captured the essential teaching of this journal: entwined and opposing forces, conscious and unconscious, light and dark, present in all primary relationships. Other works by Marlene Rudginsky can be seen on her web site at http://waterspider.go.to.

Marilyn Ditto designed the front and back covers with a sensitive aesthetic appreciation of color and form, as well as created the eloquent formatting of the text.

Barbara Branscomb, our editor, provided invaluable help in arrangement and clarity of the wording.

The concept of communicating from one's "parent," "adult," and "child" rendered in this journal comes from the book: *I'm OK, You're OK: A Practical Guide To Transactional Analysis*, by Thomas A. Harris, M.D., New York, Harper & Row, 1969.

The "square work" explained and prescribed herein is taught by Leslie Temple-Thurston, who is the founder of a non profit organization called Corelight. Leslie Temple-Thurston is the author of *The Marriage of Spirit*, CoreLight Publishing, 2000. ISBN: 0-9660182-0-6.
Website: www.corelight.org.

Illustrations from *The Flower Speaks* are reproduced by permission of U.S. Games Systems, Inc., Stamford, CT 06902 USA. Copyright 1996 by U.S. Games Systems, Inc. Further reproduction prohibited.

Notes of Encouragement

As counselors who have worked with hundreds of couples for over a decade, and as a couple who has had to do a lot of personal work as well, we have learned a simple and highly effective process to help partners work through difficult issues and get to a healthy functioning place together. The main reasons why we and the couples we have worked with were able to achieve such a coveted place are:

> *First, that we began to understand the dualistic system of being afraid of, and desiring, the same thing at the same time, namely intimacy; and*

> *Second, that we made a conscious attention shift from focusing on content (our specific issues) to looking at process (the manner in which we were dealing with our issues).*

With this understanding and attention shift, we were able to focus our work on one relatively simple task: being able to identify when we were "in our adults" and when we weren't (we will discuss this in detail in a later chapter). When partners learn how to process their conflicts and anxieties using adult-to-adult communication, the process itself creates openness, closeness, trust, respect, and accomplishment.

For couples who are in trouble, it may seem counterintuitive to think that something simple could resolve the deep, complex, and sometimes ancient issues between them — but we are witness to the fact that it can! An anchor is a simple device, yet it can hold a ship in safe harbor through a storm. Couples who want to stay together, or couples who want to attain clarity in order to make an informed decision to stay together or not, can find such an anchor in the process we explain in this book.

The natural consequence of doing this work is an increase of love, tenderness, security, joy, and contentment.

We love being a couple, and we enjoy working with couples. We believe that the primary relationship is a great, natural phenomenon, and the backbone of the family. Working on your relationship rewards you handsomely. We also believe that from a psychological point of view, choosing to do the work is your noble duty, and from a spiritual point of view, it is your sacred duty.

Healthy, happy, primary relationships are the result of skilled work. All you have to be is a competent adult to learn these skills and enjoy the wonderful benefits. The only exceptions to this are practicing alcoholics and practicing drug addicts whose minds will sabotage the work, unless they stop drinking and/or using.

This journal will teach you and your partner how to effectively work through the difficulties that arise in your relationship, or just to improve it, if that is what you wish.

The journal is designed as a workbook for you and your partner to use together to develop a deeper, fuller understanding of the value of a primary relationship, the wonderful possibilities it offers, and the inner resources you have as a couple to resolve problems. There will be both non-verbal and written exercises later in the journal to help guide your work , so we suggest you each keep a spiral notebook to have on hand. Even though many couples have similar difficulties, your journey together is unique to the two of you — the journal helps you make your own way, while benefiting from our experience and that of many couples with whom we have worked.

Our hope is that you will do the work and our wish is for your happiness together.

We recommend that as partners you read this journal together, preferably each alternately reading a paragraph aloud to the other. Take your time and discuss what shows up for you as you read together. Even if you are in a situation where your partner is unwilling to work with you, go ahead and read the journal yourself. Do the written exercises that are printed and explained in the latter part of it (because change comes from within yourself). As you understand and practice, your behavior will shift and your partner will start to respond differently. If either of you changes your footwork, the dance itself has to change.

გა

Couples:
The Primary Relationship

*I*f you were to ask people what they really wanted, most of them would put a good relationship near the top of the list. Very few people are hermits. We are built to want and need a primary relationship. It's as if we're all halves looking to be whole, to give and receive love — to be part of a circle of energy that encloses us in safety, security, and esteem. In this circle, our need is met for nurturing in the form of affection, belonging, caring, and positive regard from another. The union of a healthy primary relationship offers an optimal climate for the physical and mental well-being of children, and this shapes the emotional health of society as well. These are some of the reasons that illustrate the importance and value of developing a healthy relationship.

And you can be a healthy couple. Nothing in the universe says you can't. The three indispensable ingredients for developing a healthy relationship are:

Relationship

11 Goldenrod

The willingness of both partners to work on their issues,

&

Both partners actually doing the work together,
to resolve their issues, and

&

Both learning to understand accurately the context and
dynamics of the primary relationship.

Let's start with developing an understanding of the context of the primary relationship. When two people meet, feel an attraction, start spending time together, and starts to become exclusive, a primary relationship begins to develop. The two people become a couple. A lot happens as this natural process of growing feelings unfolds: the couple starts to feel closer — they're bonding. The desire to bond is a built-in feature of the body-mind complex. It's natural! So the process of becoming exclusive, open and close — that is, intimate — occurs naturally. The degree of intimacy increases, the desire to spend time together, to want to stay together, and to be happy together also increases.

As people spend time together and grow closer, each individual's problems are going to show up. For instance, problems such as diminished self-esteem, fear of intimacy/commitment, basic mistrust, lack of communication skills, fear of rejection and abandonment, and feelings of inadequacy can and will arise. It's inevitable. It's natural. It's spontaneous.

You can't be intimate with just part of someone — as you get closer, you become intimately involved with the whole person, including aspects that you and your partner may well be unconscious of, or defended against.

In the context of increasing intimacy, problems naturally show up. They show up to be resolved — they do not appear because as a couple you are incompatible or bad or weak or unintelligent.

On the contrary, problems occur because people are basically healthy and want to be happy. Does this seem odd? Not if you realize that a partnership can be a strong configuration for mutual help and understanding. Remember, "two heads are better than one" and on some level, we can realize that a partnership presents an opening and an opportunity to work through the problems each of us brings to the relationship — the very problems that rob us, individually, of the happiness we want.

Unfortunately, when these problems arise, we don't usually see them in a positive light. We see them as "irreconcilable differences" or "it's just not working" or "it's not meant to be" or as some other negative interpretation.

Couples can and should learn to see the problems that arise in their relationship in a positive way. The exercises in this journal present a forum for a couple to do just that — to gain a positive understanding of the internal workings of a primary relationship, to identify issues/problems each partner has, and to resolve those issues together in a context of trust and respect. As a result, both partners improve more than they ever could have alone.

In the context of increasing intimacy, a particular dynamic develops for many couples: the opposing force of fear comes into play, and impedes the natural flow of two people becoming open and close. Fear of being hurt, fear of being controlled, fear of rejection or abandonment, fear of loss of love, respect and/or esteem from your partner, fear of competition, fear of commitment, etc., can interfere with intimacy. Consequently, what we often have eventually in a relationship is the interplay of the natural conscious desire to be open and close, and the learned, often unconscious, fear of getting hurt by being open and close. Now the partners can find themselves prisoners of an apparently dualistic and opposing system, acting out a tragic emotional drama. The desire to be happy naturally brings us closer, while the fear of being hurt causes us to create distance.

Sometimes this dynamic plays out over a period of years, with the couple fluctuating between the polarities of fear and desire, essentially saying to each other, alternately: Don't get too close; don't get too far. When one partner in the couple is afraid of intimacy, usually so is the other one, and they probably both have a fear of rejection and abandonment. This is an important dynamic to understand. It is rare that just one of the partners has these anxieties, because we tend to choose to initiate and develop relationships with people who have the same fears we have.

 The unconscious mind possesses powerful strategies when choosing a mate; choosing someone with the fear of being close and the fear of being distant, which are two sides of the same coin, is quite practical. The mind is so utilitarian!

What is the practicality of choosing someone with the same fears you have? First, you don't have to be anxious about getting too open and close, because neither of you will allow it. Second, if you start feeling too far apart, you can cooperate to decrease the distance so neither of you will feel abandoned.

Unfortunately, this arrangement only works for about two or three years, after which your capacity to tolerate feeling like a yo-yo starts to diminish. The 'apparent' danger you pose to each other when getting too close, and the shaky alliance you form to keep from getting too far apart, begins to weaken the relationship and can soon break it, like metal fatigue snapping a wire that's bent once too often.

The third practical aspect of choosing a partner who has your same fears is: Since both of you have these same fears of intimacy and abandonment, neither of you can hold it over the other, and you can identify with how your partner feels. If you learn to use adult communication, you can generate empathy and compassion to resolve this rather 'cloaked issue' that you both share; if you don't, you at least get to claim judgment's booby prize, since your partner "obviously" has the problem. But please remember that if either partner's fear remains by staying hidden in the unconscious, it will rob you both of the happiness you desire.

So is there hope? Absolutely! Whether you are a couple who has yo-yoed between intimacy and distance or a couple who has taken more of a straight line from desire to disillusion-ment, your hope lies in understanding the purposefulness of this system that develops by being together.

As we've said, most people come together with unresolved emotional issues, perhaps compounded by inaccurate understanding. The baggage can show up in the form of basic mistrust, diminished self-esteem, insecurity, dishonesty, anger or vindictiveness, a victim mentality, drug and/or alcohol abuse, being overly critical or overly accommodating, and expecting to fail — just to mention some possibilities. When people get closer to each other, the baggage is un-packed, so to speak. Consequently, the contents are exposed. Once exposed, the relationship develops a context in which all the individual issues that block our happiness and inner contentment can come into view. Then we can see what they are and help each other work them through. As a result, each partner becomes healthier and more fully functional than he or she ever could have alone!

Please remember that problems don't mean the partners have irreconcilable differences, or they are bad or weak or dumb, or are punished by God; rather, problems show up in relationship because that's where help and transformation is possible. As part of being a couple, both people have an opening to work through whatever problems rob them individually of inner peace and happiness, as well as the opportunity to experience the luxury of being open and close to another human being.

If we don't grasp the purposefulness of this natural occurrence and pursue it with accurate understanding, we can start to feel helpless and hopeless. Eventually, we may exit the relationship with sadness, regret, resentment, and a sense of failure, only to move on to our next same-pattern involvement. If we choose not to work through our personal issues with our current partner, we face two probable consequences: we will either be alone, or we will replay our unresolved difficulties with someone else.

We are not saying that all couples should stay together, but rather that you might as well try to work through your problems together now, so that you can make an informed decision to stay together or not in the light of resolved personal issues.

So many couples have missed the opportunity to view themselves and their behavior with this new understanding and have never used adult-to-adult communication techniques to achieve clarity and resolve their issues. Unfortunately, we will never know if those relationships (and families) might have had a different outcome.

When you make choices, you create consequences. Choosing to do the work is all we can do, as couples, to enhance our relationship and change its course. All the rest — love, harmony, contentment, trust, and respect — will show up spontaneously as a result of the work. Choosing to be an informed, active participant helps create success, whereas choosing to be a passive or unskilled victim may cause tragedy.

Look at the divorce rate in the U.S. Fifty percent of all first marriages end in divorce, as do over sixty percent of second marriages — and that's not even counting all the couples who live together, who may or may not have children together, and who end up separating. Were all these people open and close when they terminated their relationships? Obviously not. They were distant, hurt, resentful — so they left each other.

And what about children in all these situations? What are they learning about human relationships, especially primary ones?

If separating is indeed the only resolution for a particular couple, at least let us be sure of that after doing the work, for the sake of all concerned, and let us do our best to understand each other and ourselves so as to minimize further damage. Perhaps the effort to do so will be healing in itself. Even if we become so distant we feel we have nothing left to lose, a new process may help us to see the other side of that coin: then maybe we have everything to gain.

Therefore, the aim and goal of this journal is twofold:

To help you as a couple learn how to positively collaborate to help each other resolve personal issues in order to create and maintain intimacy, and to make informed decisions; and,

৪৯

To help you become conscious of how you both have been colluding (a negative collaboration) to create distance, in order to stop engaging in those distancing behaviors.

Chapter 2

Distancing:
The Unspoken Contract

*W*orking with many, many couples in counseling, we have found that most report they are not as close as they used to be, that they are at various degrees of distance. They report feeling distant and, at the same time, report wanting to be close. Who creates the distance for couples? Was it God or country or parents? Did someone give it to them? Did it just somehow happen on its own, or turn up because of incompatibility? No! A couple creates distance together when partners are afraid of getting hurt. Fear of getting hurt is natural, but fear of getting hurt by being open and close to your partner is learned — it's learned from your relationship with your parents, from previous partners, and/or from your history together as a couple. Because fear is more primal than even desire, it takes precedence over the natural drift of moving closer thus causing partners to create distance together, without even realizing it.

Will

8   Dandelion

After a couple has been together long enough for fear to become dominant, they each learn what choices cause distance and how to create distance together. Even though consciously they want to be open, close, and happy, they unconsciously collude in distancing for self protection, making an unspoken contract without realizing it. From a therapist's perspective, it's obvious that even though the couple is having a hard time, and they appear to be adversaries, they are typically in agreement in their collaboration to create distance together.

But when people are informed that they have created where they are as a couple together, and asked what parts of themselves have made the distance happen when they really want to be close, they almost all say that they don't know. This is the truth, because the fear of being open and close with another human being tends to be unconscious, while the desire to be open and close is conscious.

Becoming intimate is the "light" or conscious half of the couple psyche, and distancing is the "dark" or shadow side. By the "dark" side, we mean that distancing isn't clear, that it isn't held in the conscious awareness. Most of the time, we can only tell we are distancing by the effect of the choice we made. For instance, if we choose to withhold affection or attempt to manipulate or criticize, we create distance. If we choose to argue about an important relational issue, rather than discuss it with mutual respect, or if we refuse to discuss it at all, we are making choices that create distance. Choices that tend to result in resentment, hurt, vindictiveness, fear, distrust, and discouragement in our partner, and a subsequent closing off from each other in the relationship are distancing mechanisms. *These sorts of choices or behaviors should be regarded as purposeful – and the purpose is to create distance.*

If my partner and I fight a lot, or avoid dealing with our problems at all, we make distance happen. We have entered into that unspoken contract, that collusion to push each other away, whether we are consciously aware of it or not. Please ask yourself and your partner if you are creating distance together, and if so, is that what you want? Only you and your partner have brought your relationship to where it is. Where you are as a couple is a result of all the choices each of you has made. Even if one of you has the active or "acting out" role, and the other has the passive or covert role, each of you is one hundred percent responsible for yourself, and fifty percent responsible for where you are together. This is true if you are both actively creating distance (e.g. arguing all the time), or both passively creating distance (e.g. you never discuss relational issues).

It's important to develop a non-blaming understanding of how this works and to acknowledge the reality that you are the cause of your own experience. If you blame others for where you are, the assumption is that they have all the power over you. If you believe that others cause how you feel — what you think, how you behave — it puts you at the mercy of their behavior. What option does that belief leave you? Trying to control their behavior puts you in a weak and insecure position. You may not even know when you manipulate, sabotage, over-accommodate, avoid speaking up, or kowtow to get others to behave the way you need them to, so you can feel the way you want. Getting clear on who causes what is really a matter of perception. Getting your perception and beliefs to accurately reflect how things are working between you and other people is well worth the effort, especially as a partner in a primary relationship.

It is said that the way we use our language shapes our sense of reality. When, as children, we hear grown-ups saying things like, "you make me" or "that makes me," we begin to believe that these words reflect accurately how things happen between people. Unfortunately, we then blame others (hold them accountable) for our experience and blame ourselves for the experience of others. As a result, this inaccurate understanding dis-empowers, demoralizes, and discourages us. It is fodder for self-pity that can and should be avoided. We cannot overstate the importance of getting clear on what you cause and what you don't cause. The resulting clarity brings true discernment which has been called the crest-jewel of knowledge.

In terms of a primary relationship, beliefs such as: "It was all my partner's fault," "It's because of the way he/she is," "If I could just be with the right person, it would all work out," set us up for another failure. This kind of thinking is clearly disproved by the statistics on the divorce rate for second, third, and fourth marriages. The pattern can't be repaired until we're willing to say: "It's not just my ex, it's me too," and then do the work to understand our part.

When both partners are willing to work on the relationship in a cooperative and earnest manner, they can get through complicated, thorny, and delicate issues and end up being closer, feeling pleased and relieved, and sharing a sense of mutual accomplishment. Even resolving minor issues can grant this experience.

A special note for couples who consider themselves to be committed: If you think of commitment as something "out there," outside yourself, existing on its own, there isn't much you can do about it. Please remember that commitment has no objective reality in and of itself – the choice of how you view it is entirely yours. If you see commitment as a prison, then it's a prison. But if you choose to see it as an opening and an opportunity, then it's an opening and an opportunity. Since nobody is in your own mind but you, take responsibility for how you choose to see things. Taking responsibility in this way frees you up and empowers you. Since you are going to stay together, you might as well see commitment as an opening and an opportunity so that it works for you in that way. Unless you have a need to suffer, it's your best bet!

If you are considering committing, make the choice you want. Don't bow to pressure or a sense of obligation from others (though freely committing from an inner sense of duty is perfectly okay). Commitment is a choice in the domain of your mind only. If you don't freely choose to commit, your mind will use "feeling trapped" as a distancing mechanism. Please remember that it's not whether you are able to commit to each other, but rather whether you are willing to commit at all that really matters.

As one couple to another, we hope that you find yourselves willing to commit at least to working on your relationship. We hope that you feel encouraged about the possibilities and that this journal will provide a safe vehicle for your journey together.

To get started doing the work, ask yourselves how you and your partner make distance happen together. For instance, a couple may create distance together when one person wants to talk about his or her issues and may pester or pressure or get angry to get the discussion going; then the other one resists communicating. Both maintain their positions. What is the result? In another example one partner is afraid to talk about his/her issues because the other is too fragile, critical, invalidating, or controlling; then silence causes resentment to build up. In a third example, each blames the other for his or her experience, or takes on blame for the other's negative experience. Blame builds resentment, and resentment is like a psychic wall between partners. Hurt, anger, distrust, fear, disrespect, and adversarial competitiveness all serve as walls between two people. These walls are always erected together, as a joint project, and are purposeful in that they aim to protect us with distance to keep us safe from the 'enemy.'

At this point, we suggest that you think about and possibly discuss the following questions.

Who or what is the enemy?

If I were open and close to my partner, how could he/she hurt me?

How do I distance?

How does my partner distance?

When you visualize you and your partner having a discussion about how you both distance, what shows up for you?

Chapter 3

Creating Intimacy:
Adult-To-Adult Communication

*I*ntimacy, as discussed in this chapter, is not about sex, but rather about how open and close you feel with each other as a couple: how safe, trusting, loving, and respectful you feel toward each other. If you aren't feeling that way together, then for you intimacy is a worthy goal. In the next chapter, we will pose more questions and offer exercises you can do together to help guide you on your way to the goal of intimacy.

Please remember that some of this work is hard because the fear of being open and close can be strong and can take many forms. For instance, you may feel discouraged even before beginning the work, or you may feel cynical about it. Feeling helpless and hopeless is in service of the learned fear of being close, not of the natural desire to be close. Whatever shows up for you when you contemplate working on getting close to your partner is probably showing up because it is being triggered by the prospect of intimacy. If you are feeling encouraged and excited, that's great. However you are feeling

Communication

Leaves ♀

about the process allows you to see where the work begins for you.

You can't be where you're not, only where you are, and where you are is your starting point. Even if where you are as a couple is not your preference, your relationship is where it is regardless of where you think it should be. At this point, where you think your relationship should be may be purely academic, because it doesn't accurately reflect where it is in actuality. If you keep laying on yourself and your partner where your relationship should be (which is where it is not), it only serves as a distancing mechanism.

So now, ask yourselves:

How do I feel about working together with my partner to be open and close?

After you have contemplated and discussed this question together, you may find it has brought up some issues for you. Start here. Communication is the only vehicle we have to resolve issues. (Of course, sometimes problems resolve themselves over time; however, more often than not they don't.)

Adult-to-adult communication, which we will explain in a moment, is the best means for resolving issues together, as you begin the process of moving towards the goal of intimacy.

There are two things involved in a discussion: the content (the issues that present themselves for you to work on) and the process: the manner in which you choose to deal with those issues. The process will determine the direction you will move in, either toward closeness or toward distance. The content (issues) will appear, you don't have to worry about that — it's spontaneous (You probably already know what's on the top of the list, anyway!). It's the way in which we choose to process the content that makes all the difference in the world. So if we process "our stuff" adult-to-adult, in the spirit of friendship and cooperation, we move toward intimacy. If we process our issues as adversaries, with distrust, hurt and resentment, we move toward distance. Please remember that in either case, we choose purposeful behaviors that make the resulting movement happen. This is how it works.

Taking responsibility for where you are as a couple means acknowledging that the two of you have brought your relationship to its present state.

ADULT-TO-ADULT COMMUNICATION

Communicating adult-to-adult is the most reliable way to resolve issues or problems. You may think relating in this manner would feel impersonal, or even artificial, but actually it is the best way to address each other. This becomes more obvious when you look at the alternatives: communicating parent-to child, parent-to-parent or child-to-child. These modes can only make the emotional tone of a difficult situation worse, and none of these is in keeping with respect and intimacy.

The following diagram depicts the various types of transactions between two people.

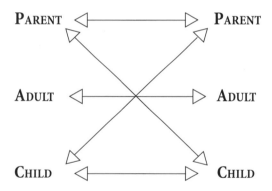

The parent mode is characterized by a critical, judgmental, or patronizing attitude, and by acting out anger or frustration with tone of voice, intensity, choice of words, and body language. This hardly opens the doors to effective communication.

The child mode is characterized by self-pity (victim

mentality), refusing to discuss important relational issues, and acting out anger, fear, and hurt through voice and body language. Again, this hardly resolves issues.

Generally, if one person begins a communication transaction in the parent-mode, his/her partner reacts with a child or parent-mode response. And, if one person initiates a communication transaction in the child-mode, his/her partner generally reacts with a parent or child-mode response. With these kinds of transactions, not only do we as a couple not resolve the issue at hand, but we also create more animosity, ill-will, resentment, and discouragement which, of course, serve to distance us further.

The place where we really need distance, and should aim to create it, is inside ourselves — if we can gain even a little distance from our own internal emotional child, and our own internal judgmental parent, it becomes easier to choose an adult response rather than a parental or childish one. With practice, we can acquire the skill to be able to identify when we are coming from the "adult," "parent" or "child" part of us. The ability to clearly distinguish the manner or mode of our communication is immensely important when dealing with relational issues.

Remember, if we engage in parent or child-mode transactions, we are choosing behaviors that will cause distance regardless of what our conscious intention may be. The adult-to-adult mode of communication, which is a level and equal form of transacting, is characterized by:

- *Respect, courtesy, and integrity*

- *Active listening (paying attention to what your partner is saying and making sure you understand what he/she means)*

- *Making sure that the words you use accurately reflect what you really think and feel, and not acting out your emotions and judgments, but rather communicating them with words, in a dignified manner, as best you can.*

It's amazing how wording something differently can make a big difference in how it's received and responded to. For instance, your partner says, "You shouldn't have done that." This tends to be parental, causing a defensive reaction. In the same instance, your partner could say instead, "I feel concerned because you did that." This tends to be adult and opens the door to talking about reasons for doing something and feelings about it on both sides.

Following, there will be some adult-to-adult communication exercises.

When communicating in the adult mode, specific guidelines help couples achieve some resolution. They are:

- *No name calling.*

- *Stick with the issues.*

- *Be very careful with, and minimize the use of, "should" and "shouldn't."*

- *Use feeling words (such as angry, afraid, pleased, sad, encouraged, guilty, worried, embarrassed, etc.).*

- *Stay away from "you make me," "I make you," "always" and "never."*

- *Use "I" statements instead of "you" statements.*

Using the format "I feel _____ because _____." helps keep you both in your adult. Put only a feeling word after the words "I feel," and then an explanation after the word "because," making one complete sentence. Then stop and let your partner respond. For example, "I feel afraid because I want to talk to you about something." If your partner were to respond using the format, he/she might say: "I feel uncomfortable because of the way you are trying to start this talk." Then you might say: "I feel sad because we have such difficulty communicating about sensitive issues." You don't have to use the format like this in succession, but it does help a great deal at times to use it this way, even though it may feel contrived.

After beginning with the format, continue your talk using the guidelines of the adult mode of communication as best you can. Please remember that if you are putting forth effort to stay in your adult as best you can, you will get better at it over time as you practice. Good is good enough; avoid the curse of perfectionism. What usually works is salt-and-peppering your communication with this format, and at times using it in succession. It will help bring you back to or keep you in your adult, whether you are talking about a particular issue or talking about how the two of you deal with issues.

Processing issues, whatever they may be, in this manner means putting effort into using words that most accurately reflect how you feel and what you think, and listening to your partner so that you "get" (understand) how it is for him/her. While you are doing this, take the position of being respectful of your humanity and that of your partner's, and maintain awareness of how fragile you may both be in this situation.

EMOTIONAL CHARGE

One aspect of communication is emotional charge, which is

the degree of intensity of the feelings conveyed by the choice of words, loudness, tone of voice and body language. Many couples find it useful to have a conversation about how to deal with the emotional charge ahead of time, when no one is upset. Discuss this when you sit down to talk about your relationship, let's say, over a cup of coffee or tea. In fact, it's sometimes a good strategy to discuss issues that you suspect will carry a strong emotional charge in a neutral setting. We know couples who discuss financial issues, for instance, in a coffee shop because they fear or know they would end up yelling at home, whereas in public they at least maintain civility.

Over time, as we continue to practice adult-to-adult communication techniques, we become fluid enough to talk about process and content in the same conversation, as needed. For instance, a couple is discussing issues they have regarding finances or sex or parenting or decision making. After a while, one or both becomes upset. At this point, to get back into their adults, each partner might try to identify the mode of communicating he/she has slipped into, and to communicate what emotions popped up and what those feelings were about. Now, they have begun talking about their process adult-to-adult. In this kind of conversation, they can release or quell the emotional charge (anger, sadness, guilt, discouragement, frustration, shame etc.) that began to pull them into their critical parent or hurt child. Now, without doing further damage, they can get back into their adults, feeling closer because they appreciate the mutual help during the conversation, and achieve some resolution on the issue(s) originally being discussed.

This exercise will help you and your partner to identify your emotional charges:

> *Identify two to five issues in your relationship*
> *that have emotional charge for you.*
>
> ૭ઽ
>
> *Identify two to five issues in your relationship*
> *that have emotional charge for your partner.*

In addition, we recommend that you make two important agreements at this time: *Make time to do the work, and, take time-outs if either partner needs to.*

CONTRACTING FOR TIME

Many busy couples, (and couples who have retreated from each other as a survival strategy) need to contract for time together to discuss relational issues on a weekly basis. Using your planner or calendar to schedule this meeting helps to highlight its importance. We recommend that a couple spend about one hour a week discussing their relationship. Also, we suggest that each of you bring an agenda with one or two points for discussion to the meeting. Anything of value needs maintenance, be it your home, your car, or your health. In the same way, your relationship deserves and needs nurturing and support. One hour a week is probably less than you spend doing yard work or laundry. Making a commitment to spend this time together is one gift you can give each other, no matter how difficult things are between you right now.

USING THE "T" SIGN

Time-out is an important process tool. For instance, if you have an issue that is quite volatile, a "fight subject," then agreeing to use the time-out sign when the emotional charge is escalating can be helpful (it can avoid a disastrous transaction). You make the agreement that while dealing with an issue of this nature, if anyone begins to flare up, one of you will make the time-out sign with his/her hands, the other will honor it, and you will both cease discussing the issue to resume it later. Part of this agreement is that whoever calls the time-out has the responsibility to initiate revisiting the issue within a reasonable amount of time.

Another aspect of time-out is that when you are going out socially, you agree on "no heavies," meaning that you want to have fun, so you agree to not bring up any couple issues.

In the next chapter, we will discuss some things to watch out for as you practice adult-to-adult communication. Sometimes when this process takes you into the woods of the unconscious we encourage you to take each other's hand as you explore what may be for you uncharted territory. We encourage you to be curious about what you encounter in yourselves and in your partner and we encourage you to give as much support as you are able to on your journey together.

Chapter 4

Working Together:
Troubleshooting the Process

INVALIDATION

Many couples complain of feeling invalidated at times by their
partners. What this means is that one or both partners are
getting the message, either stated or implied, that what they
say or think and/or feel is inappropriate, ridiculous, dumb,
not real, not okay, etc. If this goes on in your relationship, you
need to discuss it, adult-to-adult, as a distancing mechanism.
The person who invalidates someone else is rather obviously
pushing his/her partner away, but the invalidated party also
contributes to the distance if he/she doesn't speak up. If you
allow this invalidation to continue, then you are putting up
with more than you are comfortable with. By not speaking
up for yourself, you allow resentment toward your partner
and disappointment toward yourself to accumulate, thus
maintaining, or increasing, distance. This is your fifty percent
of the collusion to create distance, while your partner's fifty
percent is how he/she is treating you.

If this is a problem in your relationship, take a few moments to do this mental exercise individually:

Can you think of ways in which you feel invalidated by your partner?

Can you think of ways in which you invalidate your partner?

IMPUTING MOTIVE

Imputing motive has to do with imagining or assuming or projecting why your partner is doing or saying something. For instance, your partner asks a question like, "Why did you say that?" You assume it's not a real question and react on the basis of your assumption. You might imagine that he/she asked the question in order to criticize you, or to manipulate you, or for some other negative reason. Consequently, you start getting upset before checking with your partner to find out whether your assumption is accurate or not. Your partner, seeing your reaction, gets defensive and there you both are — distancing.

If imputing motives occurs in your relationship, discuss it adult-to-adult, and make an agreement to work on why it's happening and how to avoid it. Decide together that if either of you makes an assumption about why the other is doing or saying something, you will check it out by informing him/her what your assumption is, and the partner will honestly tell you if you are accurate or not. This kind of agreement can prevent a lot of distress, and helps cultivate honesty, trust, and integrity.

One of the amazing benefits of adult-to-adult communication is that it can transform a long-standing, hurtful problem into a vehicle for change.

IMPLIED MESSAGES

Sometimes, of course, there really is an unstated motive in what one partner says to another. We call this an implied message. Making it explicit is sometimes a corollary benefit of working on imputed motive.

Your partner says, "Why did you do that?" You respond to what you believe is the implied message, based on your partner's tone of voice and facial expression. This implied message is not stated in words, but rather in body language. The message you think your partner sent is: "that was dumb" or "you should know better" or "that's poor judgment" or "what's wrong with you?" Most often you respond defensively because you feel parented or criticized. You may, in your defensiveness, parent back, or justify and explain, or act hurt and sad (child-mode reaction). These kinds of interactions are typical for couples — negative implied messages and parent-or-child mode reactions — and they always create distance.

IRRECONCILABLE SIMILARITIES

Many couples "mirror" each other. In fact, most do when they are experiencing discord in their relationship. What mirroring means here is that both partners are feeling similarly and both have similar issues. For instance:

Both persons are feeling de-valued by their partner.

They both feel hurt and angry with each other.

They both feel less trusted, less respected, and resented.

They both care and worry about how they are regarded by their partner.

They both fear loss of love, rejection, and abandonment.

Both feel frustrated and powerless about what to do about their relationship.

Both fear intimacy, even though both consciously want it.

Both have diminished self-esteem and feel sad, discouraged, and stuck.

Confrontation/Opposition

44   Vervain   180°

Both think if their partner were only different then things would be much better.

Both are hypersensitive to the other's words, tone of voice, emotionality and body language.

Both are programming more distance together and neither of them is talking very much about all these similarities!

If a couple doesn't deal with this "mirroring," openly and honestly, their relationship may not last, or they will remain unhappy and discontent if they choose to stay together.

If the couple in the above scenario were to process (reveal and deal with) their similarities using the guidelines of adult-to-adult communication, there would be an amazing 'softening' between them such that the "mirror" would reflect closeness, empathy, and compassion toward each other.

Adult-to-adult communication is the only vehicle we have to bring us to the goal of resolution. The good news is that it's a reliable, efficient vehicle with low emissions and a high safety rating.

RECONCILABLE DIFFERENCES

Everyone is unique. Even if two people have a lot of

"mirroring" going on, we cannot expect them to be the same. Even identical twins can be very different from each other in terms of disposition, temperament, preferences, level of aspiration, etc. One could even be a Democrat and the other a Republican!

Difference between people is an aspect of reality. It is not our differences but rather how we handle them that dictates the outcome for a couple. When we have unconscious fears of intimacy, differences become a gold-mine for justifying creating distance, and of course, termination. Though differences can be a challenge, please remember, from what we've said about "irreconcilable similarities" that it's our similar thinking and feeling, rather than our differences, that usually cause relationships to fail. (Thank God we're not all from Mars or all from Venus, because then the divorce rate might be 100%!)

Protection

18 Pink Yarrow

A WOLF CAUGHT IN A PAW TRAP

Imagine that you are an "empathetic naturalist" and that the wolf is your favorite creature. You would never hurt a hair on a wolf's body. One day as you walk through the woods, you see a wolf with its leg caught in a paw trap. All you want to do is go over to the wolf, open the trap, and release it. What would happen as you got close to the wolf? How about when you reached down to open the trap? You'd probably get your hands severely bitten, especially since the wolf now associates the smell of humans with the trap set by people before you got there.

Many of us are in the position of the wolf; we feel hurt and trapped. We want so much to get out of our stuck position, but at the same time we feel threatened by someone getting close to us. That's why emotions can get so volatile, so out of control with couples. Partners assume survival mode. The stakes seem high and we behave in extraordinary, sometimes very destructive ways, which we would have never done otherwise. What each person needs to embrace is compassion and understanding for this position, not condemnation of the partner. Often, both people in the couple are stuck in this same position. It is a very painful, isolated, powerless, and mistrusting emotional place.

The only way out is to identify whether one or both of you are in this position and then discuss it openly and honestly with each other. This is a bit of a tricky situation because this kind of communication is quite intimate, which is the very thing we fear. It's often very useful to name the situation, so one partner might say, "I'm feeling like the wolf in the trap," or "I want to help you, but I feel you're behaving like the wolf in the trap."

Dealing with all these dynamics adult-to-adult, as best you can, will help you both become better tacticians at navigating the uncharted territories in the landscape of the human mind and heart. Those navigational skills, honed via your primary relationship, will help you steer a truer course in every area of your life.

The wonderful benefit of putting effort into investigating your process as a couple, whether alone, together; or together in counseling, is that it brings into your conscious awareness beliefs, emotions, assumptions, and imaginings that you were unaware of previously. The reward of this work — and it is a prize well worth the effort — is insight: an expansion of the scope of your conscious awareness. A great teacher once said, "If something is in your unconscious, you are its slave; however, once it is in your conscious awareness, you become its master."

Chapter 5

*Helping Each Other Achieve
A Positive Sense of Self:
The Bottom Line for Couples*

*A*s counselors and as a couple, we have discovered
that the root cause of the fear of intimacy, rejection and
abandonment (and the fear of distance as well) is a
negative or diminished sense of self.

If our understanding of who we are is positive, then we are
secure and confident and do not harbor the belief that, " If I
am open and close to people they will reject and abandon me
because of the way I am." It is important to address the
question: What do I really believe is true about who I am?
Many of us are plugged into negative beliefs about our own
nature such as: I don't measure up to others, I'm selfish,
dumb, bad, worthless, unlovable, unattractive, you
wouldn't like me if you really got to know me, or you'd
eventually get bored or lose interest. Beliefs such as these
cause tremendous insecurity that shows up as fear of
intimacy, rejection, and abandonment — and this is often
self-fulfilling — because, with these negative beliefs, a person

is unable to connect or bond with a partner in the way that's necessary to create a comfortable, secure and long lasting relationship.

Many people don't realize that they are identifying with negative concepts until they begin to examine the nature of their relationships, or get feedback from a partner about their disposition or moods. Investigating the question: "What do I really believe is true about who I am?", helps you uncover what concepts you identify with, and makes it possible to begin to separate who you are from what you sometimes feel, or how you may have sometimes acted. There are times, for instance, when we all feel weak — so if you tell yourself, "I am weak," you are believing that who you are and the concept of weakness are one and the same thing. This would mean that you are a concept, and a negative one at that! Are you a concept? Of course not — no more than you are a simple mechanistic mind that can entertain concepts.

Who we are is consciousness that has both body and a mind; we are not a body and a mind that has consciousness. This is a very important distinction. When a person dies, the consciousness that enlivened and empowered the body is gone. When consciousness leaves, the body becomes a corpse, an inanimate object like a rock or earth — it has no conscious awareness of being.

Consciousness is of the nature of pure awareness which is associated with light, beauty, truth, and love. This is the true nature of the self. This is who you really are, regardless of what the mind has learned to believe.

Imagine meeting someone who has never been educated at all and has had little exposure to other people. He believes that the sun goes around the earth because he can see it rise in the east and set in the west. Then you try to explain to him that, in reality, the earth goes around the sun. You might have some difficulty convincing him. Convincing someone (even yourself) out of a negative self-concept can be a little like trying to explain that the earth orbits the sun, even though it may appear to be the other way around. Nevertheless, who you are is pure, beautiful consciousness, not the body or concepts that you "appear to be" and have identified with.

It's important that you reaffirm the reality that your true nature is positive, and that you continue to do so. It may be difficult! Try saying the following aloud, while looking in your own eyes in the mirror, and see what shows up for you:

  ❧ *I am worthwhile.*

  ❧ *It's okay to be me.*

  ❧ *I am worthy of love and respect.*

  ❧ *I'm a beautiful and radiant human being.*

These statements affirm the reality of the self. The more difficulty you find with this exercise, the more important it probably is for you to do it. You can say these affirmations silently to yourself (without a mirror) thirty to fifty times a day, which will only take a few minutes.

Please remember that many people say they have good self-esteem when they really don't. Most aren't clear how they really feel about who they are, and don't want to investigate, because they believe that what they would find would be embarrassing. It could be a matter of pride not to admit that you feel negative, even to yourself, let alone anyone else. But down deep, if you don't feel good about yourself because you are identifying with negative concepts, you can never be really happy, and you will remain a prisoner of the fear of intimacy and the fear of rejection and abandonment.

We hope you see how important it is to investigate what concepts you identify with and to work on changing your understanding of who you are. Choosing to identify with positive concepts, with practice, makes a positive future possible; it also makes it easier to face yourself and deal with reality in the present. Positive concepts, like a clean, clear mirror, more accurately reflect the nature of who you are, and help reveal behaviors that are out of line or incongruent with a positive sense of self.

Couple's Journey

Exercises

Discussions

Chapter 6

Practicing Adult-to-Adult Communication: Exercises & Topics

*I*n this chapter, we will recommend some non-verbal and verbal and written exercises. You may do these in whatever order you wish; we do suggest that over time you do them all together. We designed these exercises to help you uncover the negative beliefs and fears that keep you from enjoying the naturally desirable state of intimacy.

EXERCISE 1: *Silent Gaze*

In a room alone together, with no television or music going (make sure to turn off the telephone), sit comfortably facing each other at eye level with your faces about eighteen inches apart (if you feel like you can sit closer, that's fine too!). Gaze into each other's eyes without speaking for five to ten minutes. Use a timer and maintain the gaze during the agreed upon time. Afterwards, take time to discuss what showed up for each of you. Give each other a nice, warm, long hug.

Transformation

13   Black Iris

EXERCISE 2: *Affirming Positive Regard*

Stand facing each other. Put your right hand on your partner's chest (over his/her heart) and then put your left hand over your partner's right hand. As you stand together in this position, gaze into each other's eyes and take turns saying aloud: *I cherish the love within your heart. I cherish you, I cherish you, I cherish you.* After hugging, discuss your respective experiences. You can also use this exercise to create other positive and validating messages for each other.

EXERCISE 3: *Square Work*

This written exercise is important because it deals with the polarities at the core of the dilemma that confronts most couples. This technique helps you bring into your conscious awareness the mixed feelings you have about intimacy and distance.

Please remember, if this dilemma remains in your unconscious, you will be its slave, acting it out over and over. When you bring it into conscious awareness, you will gain control over it; as a result of working on this together, both partners will gain insight, a sense of accomplishment and more closeness and openness.

In square work, we take a pair of opposites, for example, victim and tyrant, and try to flush out the ways in which each partner desires and fears each side of a pair of opposites. The idea here is to get your ambivalence out in the open. Just recognizing your mixed feelings and the beliefs you have that create them is a powerful tool for change.

Each partner works on a page to explore his/her feelings about all four sides of the square. The following page shows an example of what one partner's finished page might look like using the polarity of tyrant/victim.

Square Work

DESIRE TO BE A VICTIM	FEAR OF BEING A VICTIM
• to get attention	• it's embarrassing
• don't have to work	• it's humiliating
• security of the familiar	• fear of death
• to get sympathy	• loss of respect
• to manipulate others	• fear of no love
• playing games	• fear of feeling worthless
• bad-mouthing others	• being vulnerable
• feelings of unworthiness	• being pitied
• to avoid conflict	• meaninglessness
• feeling the need to be punished	• despair, powerlessness
FEAR OF BEING A TYRANT	**DESIRE TO BE A TYRANT**
• could be lonely	• to have power over my life
• fear of making mistakes	• to have power & control over others
• hurting others	• to get my way
• cruelty	• don't have to fear being wrong
• fear of having no friends & family	• revenge
• loss of love	• to feel superior
• being out of control	• to feel in charge
• isolating	• to get attention
• greed, hate, anger	• manipulation
	• dominance

We suggest you start by doing square work on intimacy and distance. The following pages are set up for you to do the square work. Each partner should work alone on his or her own page, filling in all four "corners" of the square. Then, take time to discuss your writings adult-to-adult. This is a wonderful exercise to expose the double-bind (don't get too close, don't get too far) situation that so many couples are in, and provides a springboard toward intimacy.

Because square work brings so much into your conscious awareness, you can use this technique on any issue to gain more clarity and mastery over it. You need to do this in writing, using the same format that is shown in the journal. Just write "desire for" and "fear of" for each of the opposites such as independence/dependence, strong/weak, active/passive, conventional/unconventional, happiness/suffering, accommodating/rebellious, agreeable/disagreeable, etc.

After you feel complete with writing about and discussing a particular square, it is time to execute the last step: letting go of or offering up the conflict or dilemma you addressed. This symbolic ritual or gesture can be done by just saying, "I now offer this up to the universe," followed by a short silence.

It isn't necessary to "fix" or resolve every conflict in ourselves or our relationships before we can be close, successful couples. Nothing is more intimate than acknowledging together the conflicting fears and desires we all experience as part of being human.

Partner A

DESIRE FOR INTIMACY	FEAR OF INTIMACY
DESIRE FOR DISTANCE	FEAR OF DISTANCE

Square Work

Partner B

DESIRE FOR INTIMACY	FEAR OF INTIMACY
DESIRE FOR DISTANCE	FEAR OF DISTANCE

Square Work

EXERCISE 4: *Topics for Notes & Discussion*

The following pages outline topics that are important aspects of your relationship. Writing notes to get more clarity and then discussing these topics openly and directly with your partner helps move your relationship to a more healthy and satisfying place.

The number of topics mentioned in this journal is, of course, not all-inclusive; once you get some practice with the method, you can apply it to any area that needs work. Please remember that as you start talking about your issues adult-to-adult, you will get better at it. Starting with less charged issues is a good idea for learning the process, and that practice will help as you confront more complicated, sensitive areas of your relationship. Work up to issues that are delicate and/or volatile.

Three important goals for your practice together are:

> *Being able to identify and stay in your adult more,
> so that you can resolve issues.*
>
> *Being able to identify and avoid your victim and
> critical parent to prevent more distance.*
>
> *Developing conversational fluidity with your partner, being
> able to talk about the process and the content as needed.*

Achieving these three goals will help you be a more happy and productive individual as well as a more secure and respectful partner. If you have children, please remember that your primary relationship is the backbone of the family and your children will benefit immensely from your work together.

We have posed some questions about each of these topics to get you started. We recommend that each of you make notes privately in your spiral notebook, or in the space provided, so that you may investigate inwardly. Other questions and facets of your particular relationship may arise for you to jot notes about, and you should feel free to do so. Think of this exercise as brainstorming, not as an essay. The notes you write can be used as a springboard for adult-to-adult discussions with your partner.

Journey Notes.........

Trust

The cornerstone of a healthy relationship.

Do you trust yourself?

Do you trust your partner?

What are some of the habits that you and your partner have
that trigger mistrust?

I could trust my partner if _____.

What are some of the situations that have happened in your
relationship that have triggered a lack of trust?

Were you trusted as a child?

Journey Notes.........

Respect

It needs to be mutual.

How did your parents treat one another?

How could you respect your partner more than you do right now? In what ways?

In what ways do you wish your partner respected you more?

Does respect have to be earned?

Do you respect yourself?

Journey Notes.........

62

Expectations
Everybody has them.

Do you expect your partner to be different from the way he/she is? If you do, please consider how this expectation could be a distancing mechanism.

Do you have high expectations of yourself (The "you don't measure up" internal message)? Write about how this could hurt your self-esteem.

Do some of your expectations or those of your partner come across as entitlements?

Do you expect your relationship to fail, or your partner to reject and abandon you?

Journey Notes.........

Decision-Making
The status balance.

Do you feel that you and your partner share fifty-fifty in making decisions in your relationship?

Do you feel parented by your partner when it comes to making decisions?

Do you feel inadequate in making decisions, and defer to your partner so as not to rock the boat?

Do you feel resentment about not speaking up when making decisions together?

Are there some decisions from which your partner excludes you?

Action

25   Tiger Lily

Journey Notes.........

66

Sex

A delicate, important & complex issue.

Who tends to initiate sex? How?

Do you have sex with, for, or to your partner?

Are there issues around sex that you feel strongly about? (For example: something goes on for you during an encounter that really feels uncomfortable, but you don't talk about it.)

Do you feel your partner would like to have more or less sex than you?

Do you feel bored with your sex life? Afraid about something?

Do you ever feel rejected by your partner when it comes to asking for sex, so you stop asking?

What aspects of your sexual relationship are working (enjoyable? comfortable? important?) for you now, or were working in the past?

Union/Conjunct

40 Rose & Lily 0

Journey Notes.........

68

Parenting

It takes work to combine differing styles effectively.

How did things change when children came into your lives?
Do you feel closer to or farther from your partner?

Are you managing to bring a family together from different
marriages? If so, try talking adult-to-adult about your concerns about the transitions. (If you run into problems, seek
counseling at the very beginning to insure that you don't allow
the transition to hurt your relationship.)

Do you feel frustrated with your children? If so, find out
within your own self what that frustration is about instead of
directing it toward the child. Can you ask your partner for
help with this?

Do you draw your children into your problems with your
partner? If so, in what ways?

Make a list of your partner's strengths when it comes to
parenting. Make a list of your own strengths when it comes
to parenting.

Wisdom

10   Daisy

Journey Notes.........

Control
Who needs it?

Who needs to control? An insecure person. Who is insecure?
Someone who has a diminished sense of self.

In what ways do you feel powerless in your relationship?

In your family of origin, were either of your parents
controlling?

Why would someone think that being in control
was necessary?

Do you or your partner have a diminished sense of self?

Do you feel that one of you is more controlling than the other?
More insecure? Is there a connection?

Journey Notes.........

72

Fear

Excitement without the oxygen.

Do you sometimes not bring up issues for fear of how your partner is going to react?

Do you sometimes have fears about the future?

What are some of the fears that show up in your relationship?

What were you afraid of as a child? Did any of your fears come true? Can you identify any present fears that are really rooted in the past?

Sometimes it's useful to compare notes with your partner as to what you think your partner is afraid of — list a few and then ask whether your perception is accurate.

Peace

32 Star of Bethlehem

Journey Notes.........

74

Anger

It is not your friend.

Do you feel angry at your partner at times, but don't tell him/her?

Are you afraid of your partner's anger? Of your own?

Is your anger more active or passive?

How do you use anger to distance in your relationship?

Are you angry with yourself (e.g., for not speaking up for yourself)?

What happened when you got angry as a child?

Note: It's good to recognize when you're angry, and perhaps to acknowledge it. However, when people get themselves more and more worked up, when anger is encouraged and indulged in, it can just get worse, like fanning a fire. We recommend that you work on understanding how anger arises within yourself in order to stop creating it.

Inner Calm

37 White Clover

Journey Notes.........

76

Regard-Valuing

We care about how our partner sees us.

Do you feel your partner lacks positive regard toward you and that it shows up through actions or inaction?

Have you and your partner ever talked about regard in your relationship and what it means to you?

When do you value your partner more? And when less?

How important is it to be regarded highly by your partner?

Does the level of caring from your partner fluctuate in your relationship? Have you discussed this openly and directly with your partner?

Devotion

22 Easter Lily

Journey Notes.........

Distancing

How far can you go?

Do you understand your part of the distancing in
your relationship?

What behaviors do you choose that create a feeling of
being less close to your partner?

What is your sense of your partner's part of the distancing?

Please share these observations with each other.

Resistance/Square

42 Dandelion & 90
Chamomile

Journey Notes.........

Intimacy

A natural, desirable & worthy goal.

Are you and your partner open and close?
If so, in what way? If not, why not?

Do you fear intimacy even though it's what you want?

Have you ever felt intimate (safe, open, close, trusting and respected) for an extended period time with another person?

What do you need to work on to be able to be more intimate?

For you, are intimacy and commitment related?

Journey Notes.........

82

Boundaries

Love thy neighbor as thyself.

Have you discussed boundaries with your partner?

How close or distant you are is the primary boundary in your relationship. What is your sense of this?

What is important about physical, mental/emotional, and spiritual boundaries?

Do you and your partner hold each other accountable for each other's experience (especially when it's negative)?

Is it sometimes hard to know where you begin and your partner ends?

Reserve

29   Violet

Journey Notes.........

84

Enmeshment

Where is it that I begin & my partner ends?

Do you over-accommodate and then resent it?

When you are making a personal decision for yourself, do you project your process of decision-making through your partner? Example: You are buying a particular item you really like, but you think about whether your partner will like it, and then you base your decision on your projection of what your partner will think rather than on your personal preference.

Is it easy for you to see things from someone else's point of view and hard to figure out what you think or want? Consider how that might affect your relationship.

Journey Notes.........

Solitude

Can make the heart grow fonder &
the couple grow stronger.

In the seasoned relationship, each person becomes the
caretaker of the other's solitude. What are the benefits of
time spent alone?

Discuss adult-to-adult with your partner the issue of balance
of time together and time alone. Do you get enough of both?

Do you ever feel abandoned when your partner wants time
alone? If so, you will need to talk about this issue.

Do you feel your partner needs to get away from you when he/
she asks for time alone? In other words is your partner
credible when he/she needs time alone for him/herself, or
does it feel like withdrawal?

Discuss how you as a couple can achieve a balance between
intimacy and autonomy.

Healing

28 Lady's Mantle

Journey Notes.........

88

Honesty
The best policy.

If you told your partner the truth, adult-to-adult and without emotional charge, how would he/she respond? (It can be useful to discuss this with each other hypothetically, without going into specific content.)

Specifically, do you have a hard time telling your partner the truth of what you really think and/or feel for fear that he/she will react in a negative way?

Do you compromise yourself about things? Example: You really don't like a particular behavior of your partner's but you don't say anything for fear of hurting his/her feelings, or of being punished.

Do you have a hard time telling the difference between the truth and a lie (in yourself or from your partner)?

Note about dishonesty: No matter how thin you slice it, it's still baloney.

Journey Notes.........

Spirituality
The sky's the limit.

What role, if any, does spirituality play in your life?

Is spirituality something you feel is worth talking about with your partner?

Are your views and your partner's views similar or dissimilar?

Beauty/Love

Flower ♀

Journey Notes.........

Processing
Can we talk?

Do you stay in your adults when addressing each other?

When you are dealing with interpersonal issues, what mode (parent, adult, or child) of communication are you generally in? What about your partner?

What is it that the child (or parent) really desires, or fears? If you are stuck out of your adult mode, try giving the child or parent its say explicitly, and enlist your partner's help and forbearance. You might say, "I know this is my four-year-old talking, but here's what he/she is scared of: _____. What he/she really needs now may be reassurance." Being explicit invites your partner to respond as an adult rather than to react from his/her own child or parent.

How can we change a negative habit-pattern of communicating?

Expression

30 Cosmos

Journey Notes.........

Friendship

A wonderful alliance.

What does friendship really mean to you?

Do you consider your partner and you to be good friends?

Does he/she usually act in your best interest?

Are you a good friend to your own self?

Journey Notes.........

Affection
Hugging is therapeutic.

Do you ever find that you withhold affection?

Does your partner ever complain that you are withholding affection?

If you are withholding affection, do you understand why?
If not, ask your partner why he/she thinks you withhold.
Really listen to what your partner has to say. When we stay non-defensive, our partners can share insights that can really be helpful.

Who initiates affection more frequently? Why?

Inspiration

14   Iris

Chapter 7

Our Concerns:
For Your Understanding

*W*e not only live our lives, we also live our times.

It's as if our struggles are all variations on a similar theme. Collectively, as a society, couples have never worked as openly and directly on being close to each other as they are now. Outer space is not the final frontier! At the same time, as counselors, we have seen that so many couples are dealing with the same kinds of stumbling blocks. We'd like to spotlight a few of the most common ones in this chapter, and then discuss what you can do if you need more help.

Many couples are still in denial about what is really going on in their relationship. Being in denial is quite a problem in itself. It means being unwilling (not unable) to look at, acknowledge, and own existing relational problems. The real tricky part of being in denial is a strong tendency to deny it. Many times, the only way a person "gets" that he/she is in denial is because of depression or anxiety or some other indicator.

Transition

31   Angelica

If we won't look at problem areas in our relationship and deal with them, they won't go away. Please remember that if you choose not to do the work, pick your ruts carefully because you may be in them for awhile.

Another common problem we often see in working with couples is that one or both partners do not speak up for themselves.

    ❧ *Do you speak up for yourself in your relationship?*

    ❧ *Do you do it directly or in indirect or cloaked ways?*

    ❧ *Which method do you use and why?*

    ❧ *What could you do to make it safer for your partner to be direct?*

Authenticity, or genuineness, is the value here. What this means is that when you are communicating with your partner, you choose words that most accurately reflect what you think and feel. Being honest in this way demonstrates integrity. If you feel afraid to discuss certain issues with your partner, start by saying, "I feel afraid because...," and then state your reason(s) as honestly as you can.

Anger, a prevalent dynamic, is something to be understood

and not indulged. It almost always occurs as a result of frustrated or unfulfilled desires. In a primary relationship, it shows up when your partner doesn't behave/think/feel the way you want; or, to put it conversely, he or she behaves/thinks/feels in ways you don't want.

Being proactive about your own anger makes you less reactive to your partner. In other words, choose to identify and communicate your anger adult-to-adult: "I feel angry because...," rather than acting it out in ways that muck up your life. Examples: depression is frozen anger; guilt is resentment directed inwardly; selective forgetting is usually anger, as is withholding affection, compliments, warmth, etc.; hostility (active or passive) is always angry; and revenge, well, you can guess for yourself.

Another facet of anger is that it is often a secondary emotion or "cover" feeling, cloaking or hiding from view the initial or primary emotion(s), which are usually hurt, sadness, fear, shame, guilt and/or feelings of inadequacy. With couples, it's common for one partner to experience the other's anger without being aware of his/her partner's hidden primary feelings. The angry person may also not be aware of the cloaked primary emotion(s). You may find it useful to ask yourself or your partner at the outset whether your anger is straightforward or an attempt to avoid other more vulnerable emotions. Working on being able to identify what your feelings are and mustering the courage to communicate them honestly to your partner is essential here. Speaking up for yourself in this way is what empowerment is all about.

Alcohol and drug use is a major problem for couples — one so serious that it's in a category by itself. Please hear our warning cry on this one! Alcohol and drug abuse can totally derail the primary relationship and, if children are involved, can create long-lasting, multi-generational tragic effects. The choices we make now create our legacy. Choosing is a responsibility that we all share as human beings.

The following questions may help you decide for yourselves whether you and/or your partner have a problem with alcohol or drug abuse:

Do you have alcoholism in your family of origin?

Do you feel that you or your partner have an alcohol or drug problem and are in denial?

How often and how much do you and/or your partner drink on a weekly basis?

Do you use or abuse prescription or non-prescription drugs?

Do you or your partner tend to get into fights when you have been drinking or using drugs?

Do you feel like you lose your partner when he/she drinks or takes drugs?

Have you ever had a time in your adulthood when drugs or alcohol have not been a part of your life?
Can you talk to one another about the drug and alcohol issues adult-to-adult, calmly voicing concerns you have about this issue?

If alcohol and/or drugs are a problem that you need support for, we recommend that you call your local AA, NA, or Alanon, and/or get counseling.

Regarding all of these common problems, please remember that the work begins with where you are. You can't be where you're not. When couples come for counseling, we ask each individual if he/she wants to work things through, feels like getting out of the relationship, or isn't sure, i.e., needs more clarity to make an informed decision one way or the other. Sometimes both parties are in the same place and sometimes they are not. Where each of you are is the starting point of the work.

In counseling, we teach couples that each partner is fifty-percent responsible for where they are together, and one hundred-percent responsible for their own self. Please remember that you are the cause of your own experience.

Neither person has any power over his/her partner to change him/her. We only have that kind of power over ourselves. Consequently, our vigilance needs to be concerned with our own mind, our own understanding and whether the behavioral choices we are making are in line with intimacy or with distance. This is the secret formula.

Within a couple, each partner encompasses feminine (yin) and masculine (yang) energies. Both are necessary for the individual, but these energies can be out of balance. Particularly in this culture, we may have an imbalance between the soft intuitive (organic) side of our nature and the more active (mechanistic) side. In other words, many of us have become human "doings" instead of human beings. We don't give ourselves enough quiet time to contemplate or observe what's showing up spontaneously within us, without any external stimulation. When we take quiet time just to be the unique individual adult we are, it improves our inner state and our sense of being a worthwhile partner. Being awake and at rest for short periods of time (meditating, just sitting out in nature, etc.) in solitude, with no external stimulation, is grounding and is pleasing to the mind-body complex. Life is much too short to not allow yourself this luxury, and it can be an important therapeutic adjunct to the work you are doing with this journal.

If the two of you keep attempting to deal with your issues,

adult-to-adult, but are unsuccessful, we recommend that you seek couple counseling. When you are ready to schedule, talk to the counselor for a few minutes and see how you feel about the interaction before making an appointment. Check out a few counselors in this way and schedule with the one with whom you feel most comfortable. At the end of your first session, if you are not sure that you want to return, it is perfectly legitimate to say that you want to think about it before rescheduling. Call after you get clear to let the counselor know your decision.

Sometimes counseling is necessary because the couple is too enmeshed, or there is too much hurt and anger with each other for the couple to get started doing the work. Counseling can provide a safe place, a forum, for beginning to unravel the surface issues, provide insight into the deeper aspects of the relationship, lend support and encouragement to both partners, and ensure fairness when dealing with the complexity.

When we work with couples, we intersperse individual sessions with couple sessions. This can be very effective in a course of therapy, because one partner may need to talk about some things that would not be conducive to the healing process if the other partner were present. Also, individual sessions are invaluable for each partner in working on personal issues such as self-esteem, fears, depression, anxiety, etc.

The goal of therapy is reached when you don't need the counselors on any regularly scheduled basis. When you have gained insight into how your mind works, have released any deep-seated negative beliefs about who you are, and have learned communicating adult-to-adult, you can carry on quite well. At this point, many clients continue on an as-needed basis, which means that if they ever feel the need for a "tune-up" session, they feel free to set up an appointment.

One last word of encouragement: getting counseling is okay! Don't buy into the belief that communicating emotions is "touchy/feely" or corny; any such idea probably comes out of resistance, which is a servant of fear. And please don't blindly buy into any other herd-mentality misconceptions. Going into counseling is not self-indulgent or selfish; it is not a sign of weakness, but an exercise in strength. When you make choices that take care of yourself, it is entirely different from being selfish. From a philosophical point of view, taking care of yourself is something you ought to do! Please remember that working towards a respectful, healthy relationship with yourself and your partner is a worthy goal; if you need some help reaching that goal, ask for it!

We hope the process you've learned in this journal will continue to benefit your relationship, through life's good times and hard times both.

Our wish list for you:

Openness and clarity in your work together

಄

A successful, inward journey towards your true selves

಄

The ability to recognize the divine virtues in yourselves
and each other, and to sustain one another as you
grow to your highest potential.

Our very best and fondest wishes,

Tony & Cristi Cubito, M.A.

www.couplesjourney.com

I saw two swans, one black, one white,
with wings of feather down outspread.
From the waters there rose a blossom pure and white.
Its crown was open and within its heart there shone a
jewel so brilliant as to almost blind me.
And then I saw that its very facets were mirrors and
that each one held a reflection of one whom I had loved.
A breeze blew gently from the south caressing my brow.
I knew then that the stone was myself and that its mirrors
were the facets of my heart reflecting to others
the many gifts of those who care.

Marlene Rudginsky

Tony and Cristi Cubito are counselors who have worked with hundreds of couples for over a decade. They love being a couple and have had to do their own personal work to develop a healthy, committed, responsible relationship. They clearly see the opportunity and value of doing the work of being a couple. With this positive outlook, they greatly enjoy working with other couples and sharing their understanding.

෴

They believe that the primary relationship is a great natural phenomenon, the backbone of the family, and that learning to be skilled workers dealing with relational issues is richly rewarding for both partners.

Couple's Journey

ORDER FORM

Fax Orders: Please send this form to: 541-686-8908

Telephone Orders: 541-686-5613

E-mail Orders: couplesjourney@msn.com

Web Site: www.couplesjourney.com

Postal Orders: Blue Pearl Publishing, P.O. Box 50248, Eugene, OR 97405

Please send me information on: ☐ **Workshops**   ☐ **Counseling** ☐ **Seminars**

☐ Please send me *"Couple's Journey"* _____ copies @ $17.95 each   *Subtotal:* _____

* Shipping: _____

Total Enclosed: _____

* US: $4.00 for first book, $2.00 US for each additional book.
International: $9.00 US for first book, $5.00 for each additional copy.

Name (Please Print): _____

Address: _____

City: _____ *State:* _____ *Zip:* _____

Telephone: _____ *E-Mail:* _____

PAYMENT TYPE: ☐ *Check enclosed*   ☐ *Visa*   ☐ *Mastercard*

Card Number: _____

Name on card: _____ *Exp. Date:* ____ /____

Couple's Journey

ORDER FORM

Fax Orders: Please send this form to: 541-686-8908

Telephone Orders: 541-686-5613

E-mail Orders: couplesjourney@msn.com

Web Site: www.couplesjourney.com

Postal Orders: Blue Pearl Publishing, P.O. Box 50248, Eugene, OR 97405

Please send me information on: ☐ **Workshops**   ☐ **Counseling** ☐ **Seminars**

☐ Please send me **"Couple's Journey"** _____ copies @ $17.95 each   *Subtotal:* _____

* Shipping: _____

Total Enclosed: _____

* US: $4.00 for first book, $2.00 US for each additional book.
International: $9.00 US for first book, $5.00 for each additional copy.

Name (Please Print): _____

Address: _____

City: _____ *State:* _____ *Zip:* _____

Telephone: _____ *E-Mail:* _____

PAYMENT TYPE: ☐ *Check enclosed*   ☐ *Visa*   ☐ *Mastercard*

Card Number: _____

Name on card: _____ *Exp. Date:* ____ /____